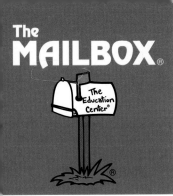
The MAILBOX®
The Education Center®

Language Arts ENVELOPE Centers

15 READY-TO-USE CENTERS

- Beginning Sounds
- Color Words
- Spelling Patterns
- Short-Vowel Sounds
- Long-Vowel Sounds
- Initial Digraph Sounds
- Ending Punctuation
- Capitalization
- Alphabetizing
- Word Families

Build Basic Language Arts Skills!

Managing Editor: Gerri Primak

Editorial Team: Becky S. Andrews, Kimberley Bruck, Karen P. Shelton, Diane Badden, Thad H. McLaurin, Sharon Murphy, Lynn Drolet, Kelly Robertson, Karen A. Brudnak, Hope Rodgers, Dorothy C. McKinney

Production Team: Lori Z. Henry, Pam Crane, Rebecca Saunders, Jennifer Tipton Cappoen, Chris Curry, Sarah Foreman, Theresa Lewis Goode, Clint Moore, Greg D. Rieves, Barry Slate, Donna K. Teal, Zane Williard, Tazmen Carlisle, Marsha Heim, Lynette Dickerson, Mark Rainey

www.themailbox.com

Another Fine Product From the Learning Centers Club®

Table of Contents

15 Envelope Centers

Skill

©2006 The Mailbox®
All rights reserved.
ISBN10 #1-56234-707-1 • ISBN13 #978-156234-707-9

Manufactured in the United States
10 9 8 7 6 5 4 3 2 1

How to Use

1. Read the teacher directions for each envelope center and prepare the center as directed.

2. Use the center as directed on the teacher page to reinforce the corresponding skills you are teaching.

3. Use the center as independent practice or for early finishers. If desired, send a center home with a student for additional practice.

4. Use the checklist on page 4 to help keep track of each student's progress.

Teacher Directions

Envelope Center

Center Mat

Targeted Language Arts Skill

Student Directions

Center Cards

Practice Page

Envelope Center Checklist

Student	Wobbling Towers: Identifying beginning sounds /t/ and /w/	Trail Buddies: Identifying beginning sounds /b/ and /r/	Mail Call! Matching beginning sounds to the letters *c* and *h*	Candy Galore: Matching beginning sounds to the letters *n* and *p*	Order Up! Matching beginning sounds to the letters *d* and *s*	Kitty's Choice: Matching color words	Monster Movie: Spelling of CVC words	To the Moon! Identifying short-vowel sounds /a/, /e/, and /o/	Queen of the Castle: Identifying long-vowel sounds /a/ and /i/	Strike a Pose! Identifying initial digraph sounds: /sh/, /th/, and /wh/	Suds for Sam: Ending punctuation—asking and telling sentences	Collecting Carrots: Capitalization	The Banana Express: Alphabetizing words to the first letter	Rainy Day Snake: Word families: *-ain*, *-ake*	Mice on the Vine: Word families: *-ice*, *-ine*

Wobbling Towers

Pages 5–12

Materials:

scissors
glue
10" x 13" envelope
resealable plastic bag

Preparing the center:

1. Tear out the student directions, center mat, and center cards on pages 7–12.
2. Glue the student directions (page 7) on the envelope. If desired, laminate the center mat and cards on pages 9–12.
3. Cut out the cards and place them in the bag.
4. Make copies of the reproducible practice page on page 6.
5. Store the center mat, bag, and copies of the practice page inside the envelope.

Using the center:

Have the student follow the directions on the envelope. Provide assistance as needed. After she completes the center activity, have the student complete a copy of the practice page.

Wobbling Towers

✂ Cut.   Glue to match beginning sounds.

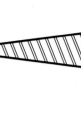 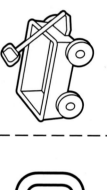  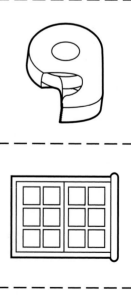

Note to the teacher: Use with the directions on page 5.

Wobbling Towers

Here's what you do:

1. Sort by beginning sounds.

2. Check.

Wobbling Towers

Wobbling Towers

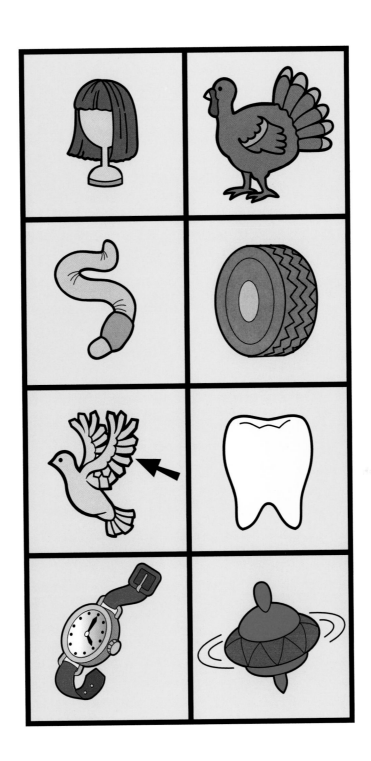

Wobbling Towers
TEC61029

Wobbling Towers
TEC61029

Wobbling Towers
TEC61029

Wobbling Towers
TEC61029

Wobbling Towers
TEC61029

Wobbling Towers
TEC61029

Wobbling Towers
TEC61029

Wobbling Towers
TEC61029

Trail Buddies

Pages 13–20

Materials:

scissors
glue
10" x 13" envelope
resealable plastic bag

Preparing the center:

1. Tear out the student directions, center mat, and center cards on pages 15–20.
2. Glue the student directions (page 15) on the envelope. If desired, laminate the center mat and cards on pages 17–20.
3. Cut out the cards and place them in the bag.
4. Make copies of the reproducible practice page on page 14.
5. Store the center mat, bag, and copies of the practice page inside the envelope.

Using the center:

Have the student follow the directions on the envelope. Provide assistance as needed. After she completes the center activity, have the student complete a copy of the practice page.

Name _____

Trail Buddies

✂ Cut.

Glue to match beginning sounds.

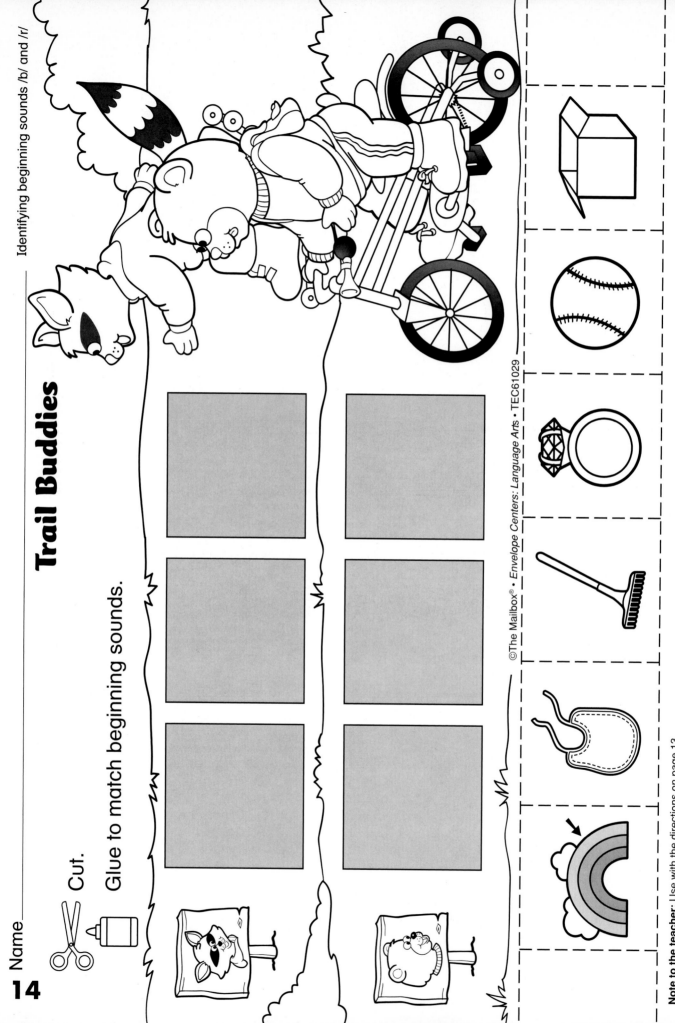

Note to the teacher: Use with the directions on page 13.

14

Trail Buddies

Here's what you do:

1. Sort by beginning sounds.

2. Check.

Trail Buddies

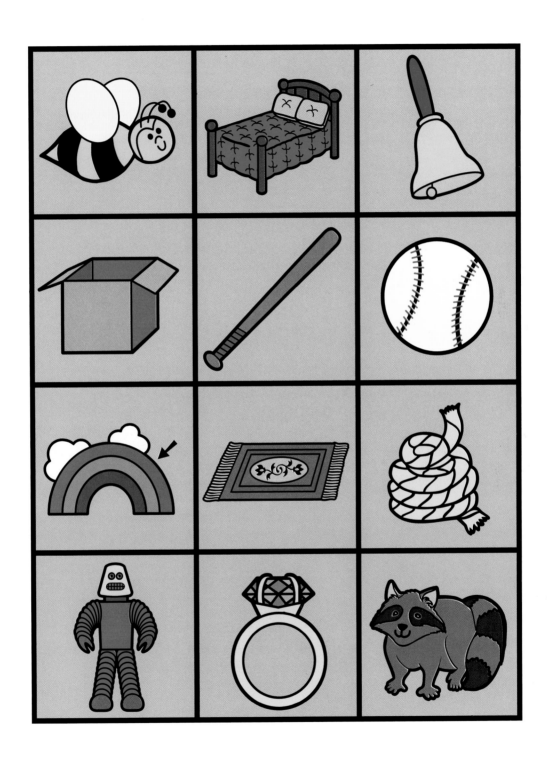

Trail Buddies
TEC61029

Trail Buddies
TEC61029

Trail Buddies
TEC61029

Trail Buddies
TEC61029

Trail Buddies
TEC61029

Trail Buddies
TEC61029

Trail Buddies
TEC61029

Trail Buddies
TEC61029

Trail Buddies
TEC61029

Trail Buddies
TEC61029

Trail Buddies
TEC61029

Trail Buddies
TEC61029

Mail Call!

Pages 21–28

Materials:

scissors
glue
10" x 13" envelope
resealable plastic bag

Preparing the center:

1. Tear out the student directions, center mat, and center cards on pages 23–28.
2. Glue the student directions (page 23) on the envelope. If desired, laminate the center mat and cards on pages 25–28.
3. Cut out the cards and place them in the bag.
4. Make copies of the reproducible practice page on page 22.
5. Store the center mat, bag, and copies of the practice page inside the envelope.

Using the center:

Have the student follow the directions on the envelope. Provide assistance as needed. After he completes the center activity, have the student complete a copy of the practice page.

Name _____

Mail Call!

Name each picture.

Color by the code.

Color Code
c—orange
h—green

©The Mailbox® • *Envelope Centers: Language Arts* • TEC61029

22 **Note to the teacher:** Use with the directions on page 21.

Mail Call!

Here's what you do:

1. Sort each card onto a mailbox.

2. Check.

Mail Call!

h

c

©The Mailbox® *Envelope Centers: Language Arts* • TEC61029

Mail Call!

h

Mail Call!
TEC61029

h

Mail Call!
TEC61029

h

Mail Call!
TEC61029

h

Mail Call!
TEC61029

h

Mail Call!
TEC61029

h

Mail Call!
TEC61029

c

Mail Call!
TEC61029

c

Mail Call!
TEC61029

c

Mail Call!
TEC61029

c

Mail Call!
TEC61029

c

Mail Call!
TEC61029

c

Mail Call!
TEC61029

Candy Galore

Pages 29–36

Materials:

scissors
glue
10" x 13" envelope
resealable plastic bag

Preparing the center:

1. Tear out the student directions, center mat, and center cards on pages 31–36.
2. Glue the student directions (page 31) on the envelope. If desired, laminate the center mat and cards on pages 33–36.
3. Cut out the cards and place them in the bag.
4. Make copies of the reproducible practice page on page 30.
5. Store the center mat, bag, and copies of the practice page inside the envelope.

Using the center:

Have the student follow the directions on the envelope. Provide assistance as needed. After she completes the center activity, have the student complete a copy of the practice page.

Candy Galore

Name each picture.

Color by the code.

Color Code
n—red
p—yellow

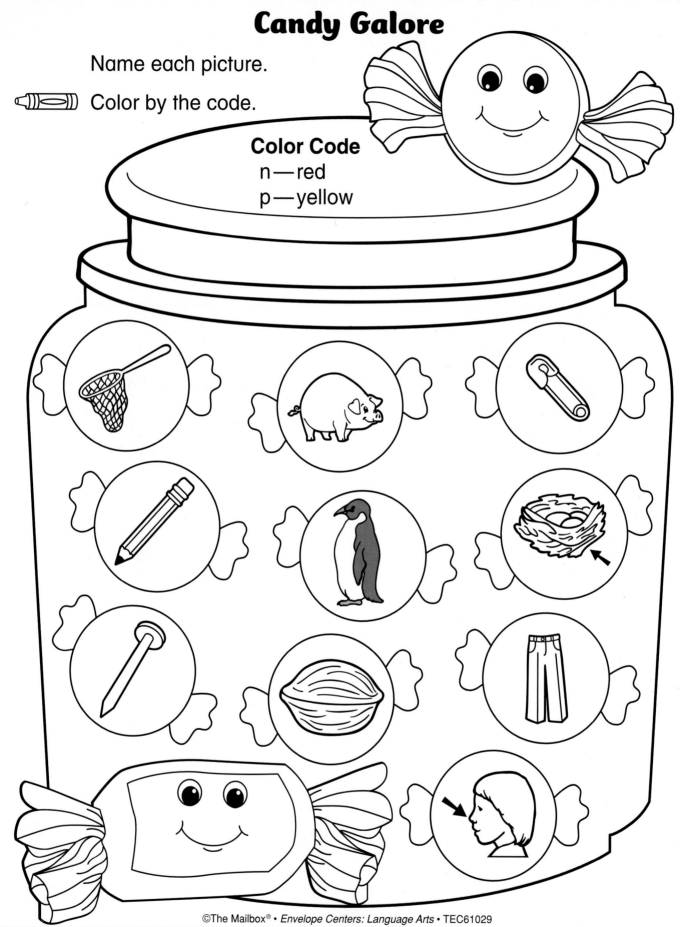

©The Mailbox® • *Envelope Centers: Language Arts* • TEC61029

30 **Note to the teacher:** Use with the directions on page 29.

Candy Galore

Here's what you do:

1. Sort each card onto a jar.

2. Check.

Candy Galore

Candy Galore

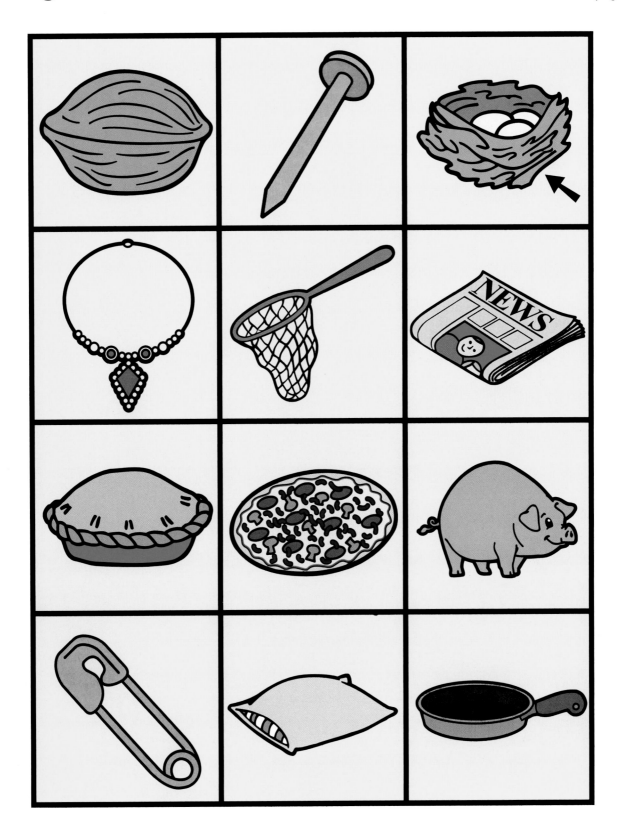

n

Candy Galore
TEC61029

n

Candy Galore
TEC61029

n

Candy Galore
TEC61029

n

Candy Galore
TEC61029

n

Candy Galore
TEC61029

n

Candy Galore
TEC61029

p

Candy Galore
TEC61029

p

Candy Galore
TEC61029

p

Candy Galore
TEC61029

p

Candy Galore
TEC61029

p

Candy Galore
TEC61029

p

Candy Galore
TEC61029

Order Up!

Pages 37–44

Materials:

scissors
glue
10" x 13" envelope
resealable plastic bag

Preparing the center:

1. Tear out the student directions, center mat, and center cards on pages 39–44.
2. Glue the student directions (page 39) on the envelope. If desired, laminate the center mat and cards on pages 41–44.
3. Cut out the cards and place them in the bag.
4. Make copies of the reproducible practice page on page 38.
5. Store the center mat, bag, and copies of the practice page inside the envelope.

Using the center:

Have the student follow the directions on the envelope. Provide assistance as needed. After he completes the center activity, have the student complete a copy of the practice page.

Order Up!

Matching beginning sounds to the letters *d* and *s*

✂ Cut. ⬜ Glue to match the pictures and the beginning letters.

s

d

©The Mailbox® • *Envelope Centers: Language Arts* • TEC61029

Note to the teacher: Use with the directions on page 37.

Order Up!

Here's what you do:

1. Sort each card onto a carton.

2. Check.

KETCHUP

Order Up!

Order Up!

d

Order Up!
TEC61029

d

Order Up!
TEC61029

d

Order Up!
TEC61029

d

Order Up!
TEC61029

d

Order Up!
TEC61029

d

Order Up!
TEC61029

s

Order Up!
TEC61029

s

Order Up!
TEC61029

s

Order Up!
TEC61029

s

Order Up!
TEC61029

s

Order Up!
TEC61029

s

Order Up!
TEC61029

Kitty's Choice

Pages 45–52

Materials:

scissors
glue
10" x 13" envelope
resealable plastic bag

Preparing the center:

1. Tear out the student directions, center mat, and center cards on pages 47–52.
2. Glue the student directions (page 47) on the envelope. If desired, laminate the center mat and cards on pages 49–52.
3. Cut out the cards and place them in the bag.
4. Make copies of the reproducible practice page on page 46.
5. Store the center mat, bag, and copies of the practice page inside the envelope.

Using the center:

Have the student follow the directions on the envelope. Provide assistance as needed. After she completes the center activity, have the student complete a copy of the practice page.

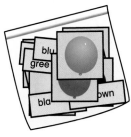

Kitty's Choice

Color.

brown

blue

orange

green

purple

red

yellow

black

Balloons for Sale

Note to the teacher: Use with the directions on page 45.

Kitty's Choice

Here's what you do:

1. Put a balloon card on the mat.

2. Put the matching color word on the mat.

3. Check.

4. Repeat.

Balloons For Sale

Kitty's Choice

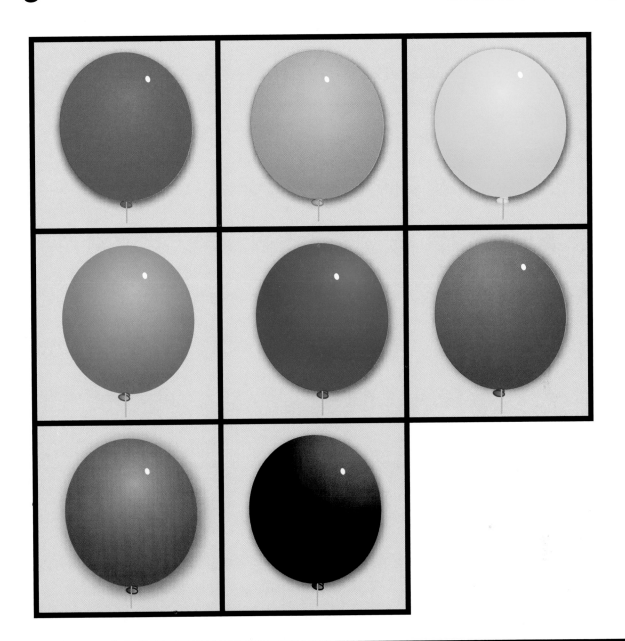

red	orange	yellow
green	blue	purple
brown	black	

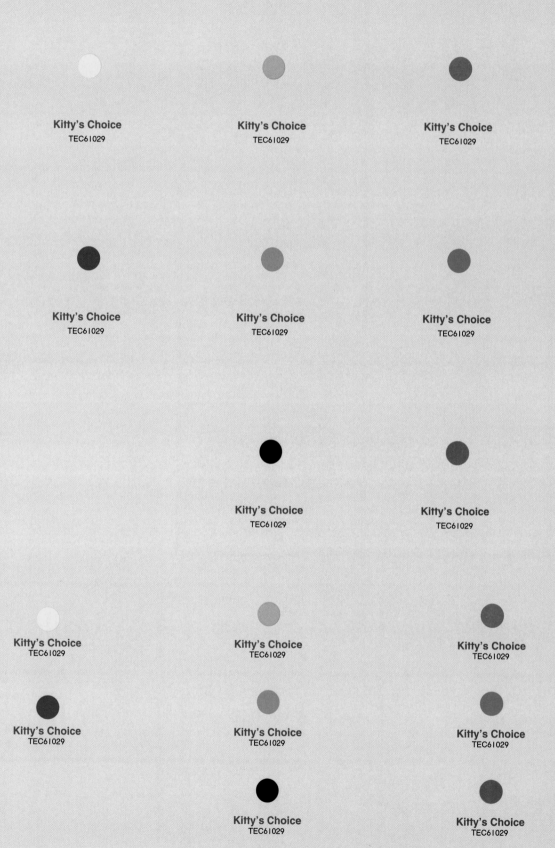

Kitty's Choice
TEC61029

Kitty's Choice
TEC61029

Kitty's Choice
TEC61029

Kitty's Choice
TEC61029

Kitty's Choice
TEC61029

Kitty's Choice
TEC61029

Kitty's Choice
TEC61029

Kitty's Choice
TEC61029

Kitty's Choice
TEC61029

Kitty's Choice
TEC61029

Kitty's Choice
TEC61029

Kitty's Choice
TEC61029

Kitty's Choice
TEC61029

Kitty's Choice
TEC61029

Kitty's Choice
TEC61029

Monster Movie

Pages 53–62

Materials:

scissors
glue
10" x 13" envelope
2 resealable plastic bags

Preparing the center:

1. Tear out the student directions, center mat, and center cards on pages 55–62.
2. Glue the student directions (page 55) on the envelope. If desired, laminate the center mat and cards on pages 57–62.
3. Cut out the cards and place the picture cards and letter cards in separate bags.
4. Make copies of the reproducible practice page on page 54.
5. Store the center mat, bags, and copies of the practice page inside the envelope.

Using the center:

Have the student follow the directions on the envelope. Provide assistance as needed. After she completes the center activity, have the student complete a copy of the practice page.

Monster Movie

✏️ Finish writing each word.

___ a ___

___ i ___

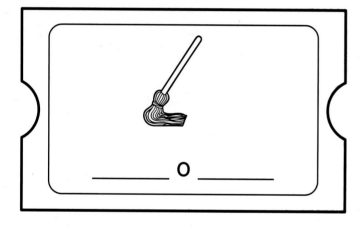

___ o ___

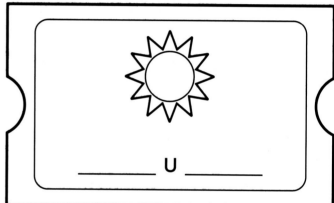

___ U ___

___ a ___

Monster Movie

Here's what you do:

1. Put a picture on the mat.

2. Put letters on the mat to spell the word.

3. Check. Remove the cards.

4. Repeat.

Tickets

Now Showing
Sleepy
Ugly

Monster Movie

Monster Movie

_____ a _____	_____ a _____	_____ a _____
_____ a _____	_____ i _____	_____ i _____
_____ i _____	_____ o _____	_____ o _____
_____ o _____	_____ u _____	_____ u _____

hat

bat

cat

pig

dig

mat

mop

hop

wig

bun

sun

top

Monster Movie

a	b	c
d	g	h
i	m	n
o	p	s
t	u	w

Monster Movie
TEC61029

Monster Movie
TEC61029

Monster Movie
TEC61029

Monster Movie
TEC61029

Monster Movie
TEC61029

Monster Movie
TEC61029

Monster Movie
TEC61029

Monster Movie
TEC61029

Monster Movie
TEC61029

Monster Movie
TEC61029

Monster Movie
TEC61029

Monster Movie
TEC61029

Monster Movie
TEC61029

Monster Movie
TEC61029

Monster Movie
TEC61029

To the Moon!

Pages 63–72

Materials:

scissors
glue
10" x 13" envelope
resealable plastic bag

Preparing the center:

1. Tear out the student directions, center mat, and center cards on pages 65–72.
2. Glue the student directions (page 65) on the envelope. If desired, laminate the center mat and cards on pages 67–72.
3. Cut out the cards and place them in the bag.
4. Make copies of the reproducible practice page on page 64.
5. Store the center mat, bag, and copies of the practice page inside the envelope.

Using the center:

Have the student follow the directions on the envelope. Provide assistance as needed. After he completes the center activity, have the student complete a copy of the practice page.

Name _____

To the Moon!

Color each star by the code.

Color Code

ă as in 🐱—yellow

ĕ as in 🐶—orange

ŏ as in 🐕—purple

Note to the teacher: Use with the directions on page 63.

To the Moon!

Here's what you do:

1. Sort the cards by vowel sounds.

2. Check.

To the Moon!

ă

ŏ

ĕ

To the Moon!

To the Moon!
TEC61029

To the Moon!
TEC61029

To the Moon!
TEC61029

To the Moon!
TEC61029

To the Moon!
TEC61029

To the Moon!
TEC61029

To the Moon!
TEC61029

To the Moon!
TEC61029

To the Moon!
TEC61029

To the Moon!
TEC61029

To the Moon!
TEC61029

To the Moon!
TEC61029

To the Moon!

To the Moon!
TEC61029

To the Moon!
TEC61029

To the Moon!
TEC61029

To the Moon!
TEC61029

To the Moon!
TEC61029

To the Moon!
TEC61029

To the Moon!
TEC61029

To the Moon!
TEC61029

To the Moon!
TEC61029

To the Moon!
TEC61029

To the Moon!
TEC61029

To the Moon!
TEC61029

Queen of the Castle

Pages 73–80

Materials:

scissors
glue
10" x 13" envelope
resealable plastic bag

Preparing the center:

1. Tear out the student directions, center mat, and center cards on pages 75–80.
2. Glue the student directions (page 75) on the envelope. If desired, laminate the center mat and cards on pages 77–80.
3. Cut out the cards and place them in the bag.
4. Make copies of the reproducible practice page on page 74.
5. Store the center mat, bag, and copies of the practice page inside the envelope.

Using the center:

Have the student follow the directions on the envelope. Provide assistance as needed. After she completes the center activity, have the student complete a copy of the practice page.

Name _____

Queen of the Castle

 Cut.

Glue to match the vowel sounds.

Write.

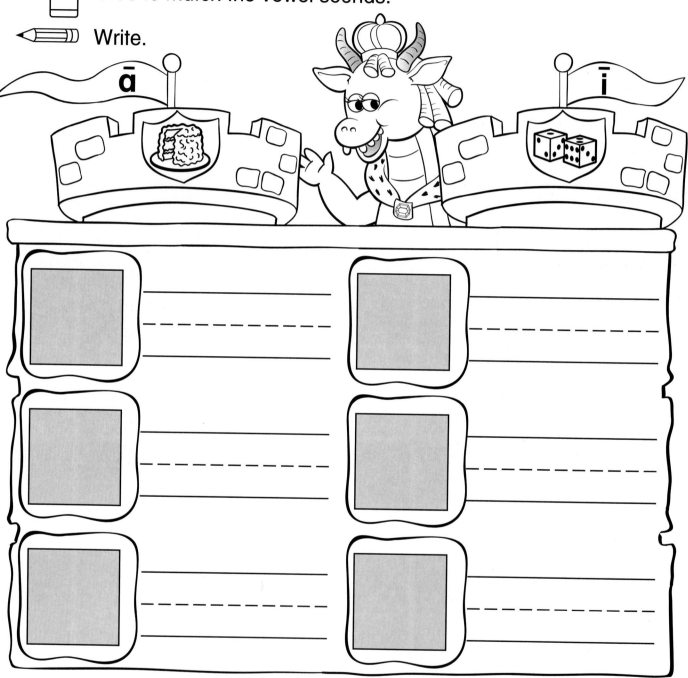

ā   ī

©The Mailbox® • Envelope Centers: Language Arts • TEC61029

Note to the teacher: Use with the directions on page 73.

Queen of the Castle

Here's what you do:

1. Sort the picture cards by vowel sounds.

2. Match each word card to its picture.

3. Check.

Queen of the Castle

Queen of the Castle

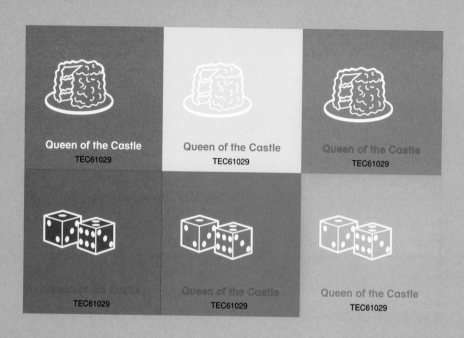

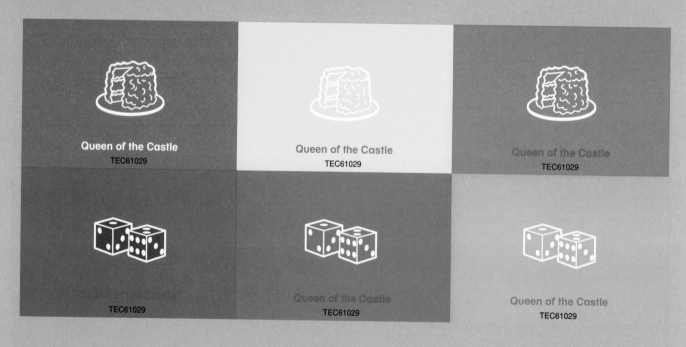

Strike a Pose!

Pages 81–88

Materials:

scissors
glue
10" x 13" envelope
resealable plastic bag

Preparing the center:

1. Tear out the student directions, center mat, and center cards on pages 83–88.
2. Glue the student directions (page 83) on the envelope. If desired, laminate the center mat and cards on pages 85–88.
3. Cut out the cards and place them in the bag.
4. Make copies of the reproducible practice page on page 82.
5. Store the center mat, bag, and copies of the practice page inside the envelope.

Using the center:

Have the student follow the directions on the envelope. Provide assistance as needed. After he completes the center activity, have the student complete a copy of the practice page.

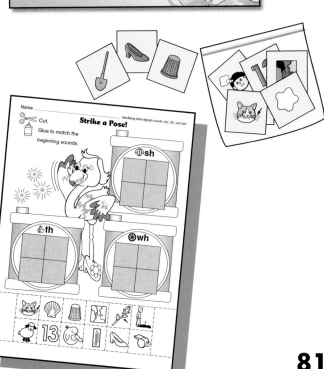

81

Name _____

Strike a Pose!

✂ Cut.

Glue to match the

beginning sounds.

©The Mailbox® • *Envelope Centers: Language Arts* • TEC61029

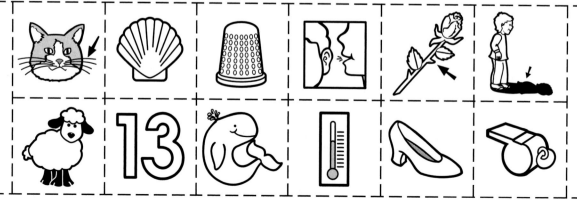

Note to the teacher: Use with the directions on page 81.

Strike a Pose!

Here's what you do:

1. Sort by beginning sounds.

2. Check.

Strike a Pose!

wh

th

sh

Strike a Pose!

Strike a Pose!
TEC61029

Strike a Pose!
TEC61029

Strike a Pose!
TEC61029

Strike a Pose!
TEC61029

Strike a Pose!
TEC61029

Strike a Pose!
TEC61029

Strike a Pose!
TEC61029

Strike a Pose!
TEC61029

Strike a Pose!
TEC61029

Strike a Pose!
TEC61029

Strike a Pose!
TEC61029

Strike a Pose!
TEC61029

Strike a Pose!
TEC61029

Strike a Pose!
TEC61029

Strike a Pose!
TEC61029

Suds for Sam

Pages 89–96

Materials:

scissors
glue
10" x 13" envelope
resealable plastic bag

Preparing the center:

1. Tear out the student directions, center mat, and center cards on pages 91–96.
2. Glue the student directions (page 91) on the envelope. If desired, laminate the center mat and cards on pages 93–96.
3. Cut out the cards and place them in the bag.
4. Make copies of the reproducible practice page on page 90.
5. Store the center mat, bag, and copies of the practice page inside the envelope.

Using the center:

Have the student follow the directions on the envelope. Provide assistance as needed. After she completes the center activity, have the student complete a copy of the practice page.

Suds for Sam

✏️ Write a **.** or **?** in each box.

🖍️ Color a matching bubble.

1. Sam fills the tub with water ☐

2. He takes a bath in the tub ☐

3. Will Sam sing in the tub ☐

4. What song will he sing ☐

5. Where is his soap ☐

6. The soap smells very good ☐

7. Does Sam smell good ☐

8. Sam is very clean now ☐

Note to the teacher: Use with the directions on page 89.

Suds for Sam

Here's what you do:

1. Put a sentence on the tub.

2. Add the correct punctuation mark.

3. Check. Remove the cards.

4. Repeat.

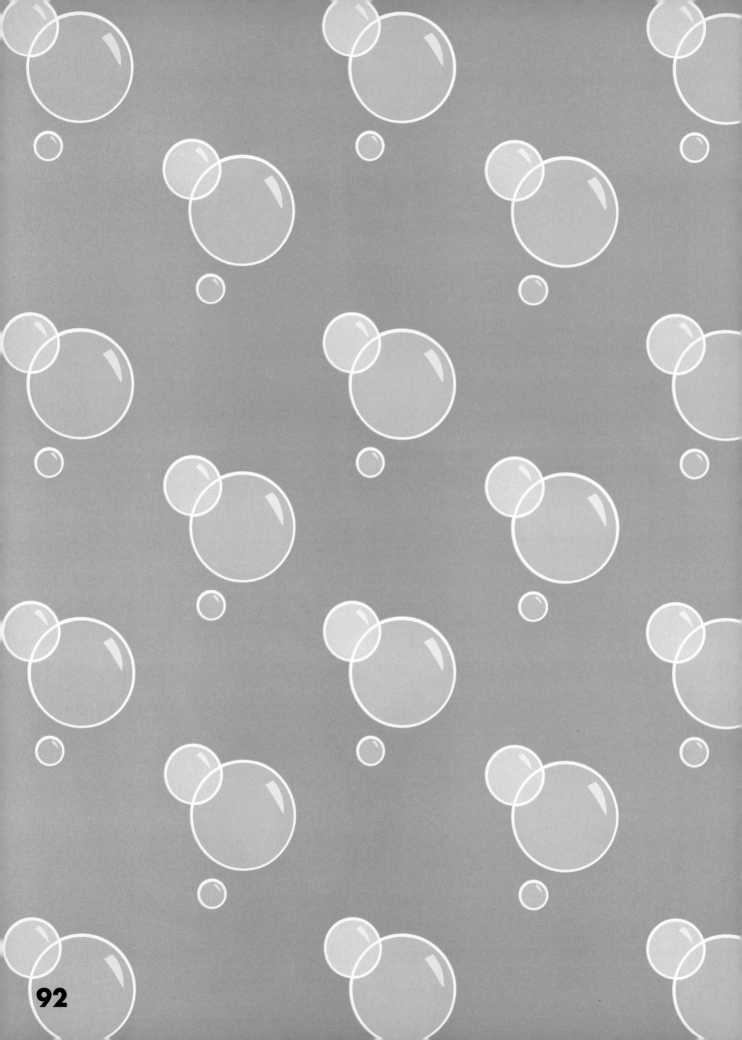

Suds for Sam

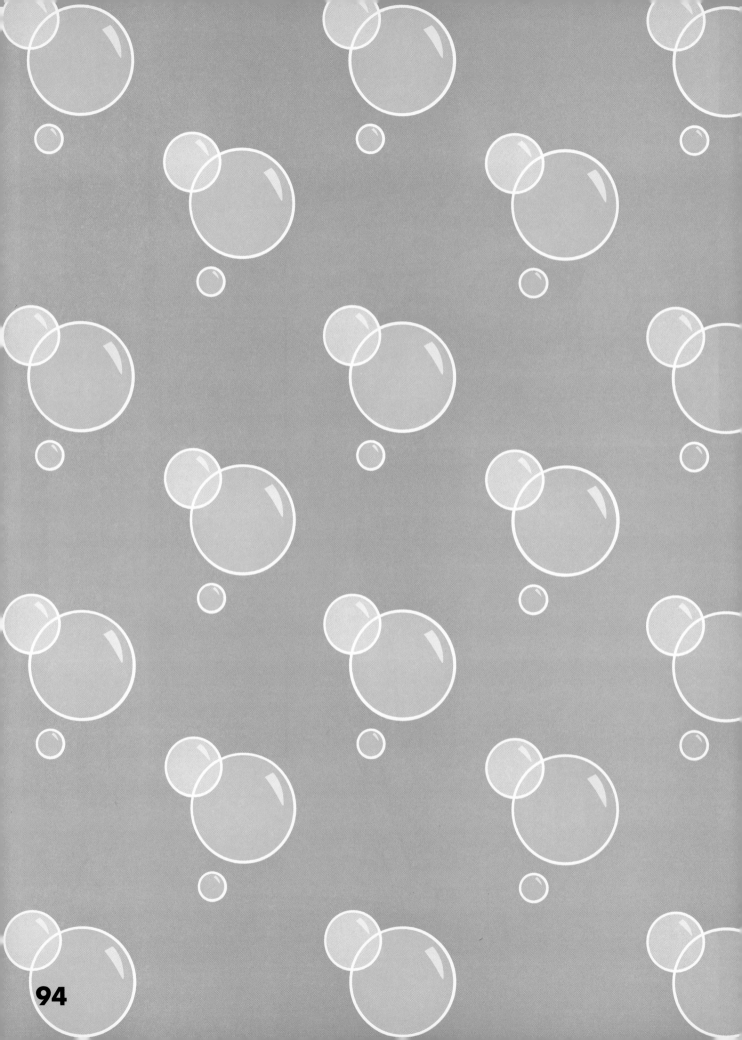

Suds for Sam

Sam likes bubbles

Sam washes his feet

Does Sam like bubbles

Will Sam wash his feet

?

.

There is a yellow duck

The water is hot

Is the duck yellow

Is the water hot

Sam is in the tub

The soap is pink

Who is in the tub

What color is Sam's soap

Suds for Sam
TEC61029

Suds for Sam
TEC61029

Suds for Sam
TEC61029

Suds for Sam
TEC61029

Suds for Sam
TEC61029

Suds for Sam
TEC61029

Suds for Sam
TEC61029

Suds for Sam
TEC61029

Suds for Sam
TEC61029

Suds for Sam
TEC61029

Suds for Sam
TEC61029

Suds for Sam
TEC61029

Collecting Carrots

Pages 97–104

Materials:

scissors
glue
10" x 13" envelope
resealable plastic bag
writing paper

Preparing the center:

1. Tear out the student directions, center mat, and center cards on pages 99–104.
2. Glue the student directions (page 99) on the envelope. If desired, laminate the center mat and cards on pages 101–104.
3. Cut out the cards and place them in the bag.
4. Make copies of the reproducible practice page on page 98.
5. Store the center mat, bag, paper, and copies of the practice page inside the envelope.

Using the center:

Have the student follow the directions on the envelope. Provide assistance as needed. After he completes the center activity, have the student complete a copy of the practice page.

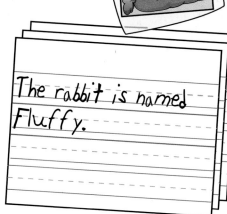

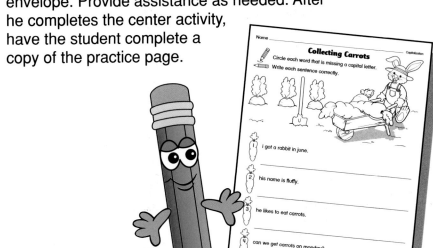

Collecting Carrots

 Circle each word that is missing a capital letter.

 Write each sentence correctly.

 **1** i got a rabbit in june.

_____

 **2** his name is fluffy.

_____

 **3** he likes to eat carrots.

_____

 **4** can we get carrots on monday?

_____

Note to the teacher: Use with the directions on page 97.

Collecting Carrots

Here's what you do:

1. Take a carrot.

2. Write the sentence on your paper.

3. Capitalize where needed.

4. Check. If your sentence is correct, put the carrot on the wagon.

5. Repeat.

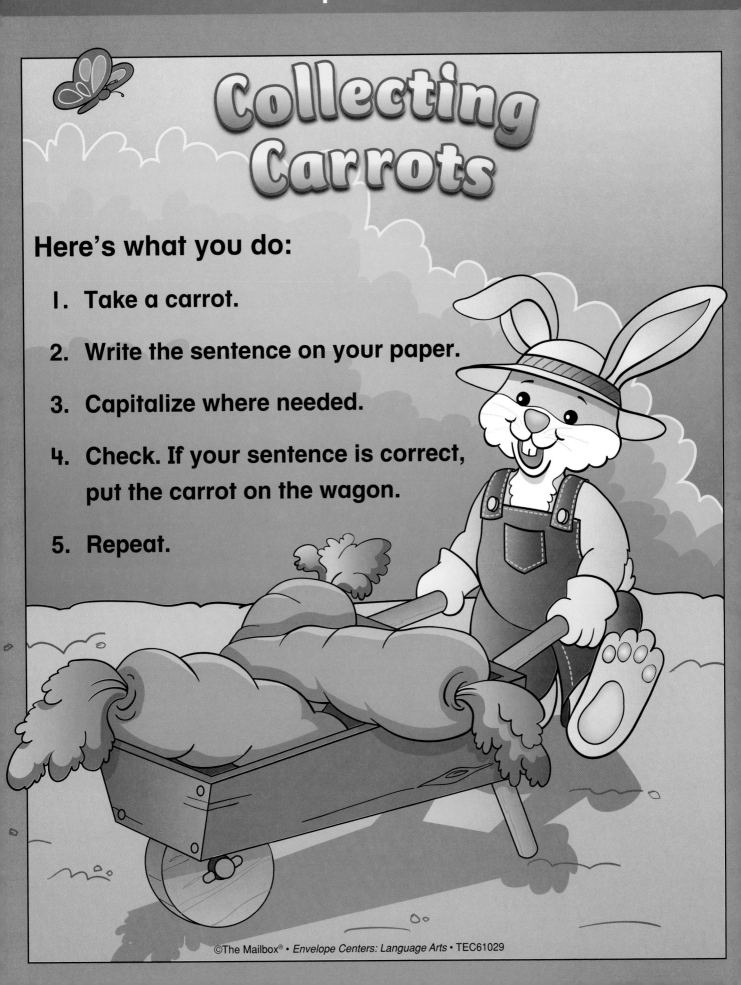

Collecting Carrots

Collecting Carrots

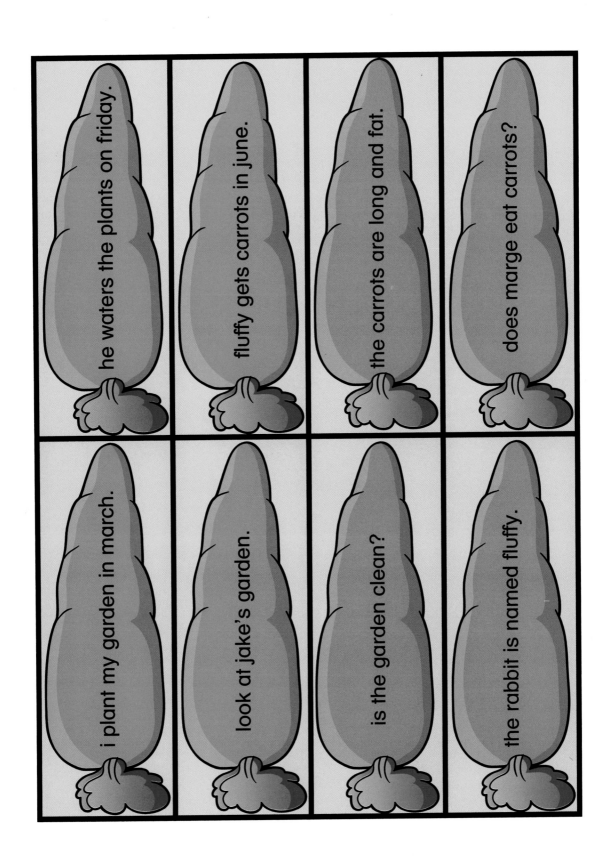

he waters the plants on friday.

fluffy gets carrots in june.

the carrots are long and fat.

does marge eat carrots?

i plant my garden in march.

look at jake's garden.

is the garden clean?

the rabbit is named fluffy.

He waters the plants on Friday.

I plant my garden in March.

Fluffy gets carrots in June.

Look at Jake's garden.

The carrots are long and fat.

Is the garden clean?

Does Marge eat carrots?

The rabbit is named Fluffy.

The Banana Express

Pages 105–112

Materials:

scissors
glue
10" x 13" envelope
resealable plastic bag

Preparing the center:

1. Tear out the student directions, center mat, and center cards on pages 107–112.
2. Glue the student directions (page 107) on the envelope. If desired, laminate the center mat and cards on pages 109–112.
3. Cut out the cards and place them in the bag.
4. Make copies of the reproducible practice page on page 106.
5. Store the center mat, bag, and copies of the practice page inside the envelope.

Using the center:

Have the student follow the directions on the envelope. Provide assistance as needed. After she completes the center activity, have the student complete a copy of the practice page.

Name _____

106

The Banana Express

Write each group of words in ABC order.

happy
apple
duck

time
bat
side

water
jam
lock

1. _____

2. _____

3. _____

1. _____

2. _____

3. _____

1. _____

2. _____

3. _____

Note to the teacher: Use with the directions on page 105.

The Banana Express

Here's what you do:

1. Choose one color of cards.

2. Put them in ABC order.

3. Check.

4. Repeat.

The Banana Express

The Banana Express

cat	girl	nice
bus	man	top
ham	people	van
friend	lip	sad

3

2

I

The Banana Express
TEC61029

The Banana Express
TEC61029

The Banana Express
TEC61029

3

2

I

The Banana Express
TEC61029

The Banana Express
TEC61029

The Banana Express
TEC61029

3

2

I

The Banana Express
TEC61029

The Banana Express
TEC61029

The Banana Express
TEC61029

3

2

I

The Banana Express
TEC61029

The Banana Express
TEC61029

The Banana Express
TEC61029

Rainy Day Snake

Pages 113–120

Materials:

scissors
glue
10" x 13" envelope
resealable plastic bag

Preparing the center:

1. Tear out the student directions, center mat, and center cards on pages 115–120.
2. Glue the student directions (page 115) on the envelope. If desired, laminate the center mat and cards on pages 117–120.
3. Cut out the cards and place them in the bag.
4. Make copies of the reproducible practice page on page 114.
5. Store the center mat, bag, and copies of the practice page inside the envelope.

Using the center:

Have the student follow the directions on the envelope. Provide assistance as needed. After he completes the center activity, have the student complete a copy of the practice page.

Rainy Day Snake

✂️ Cut.

Glue to match the word family.

✏️ Write.

-ain

-ake

Note to the teacher: Use with the directions on page 113.

Rainy Day Snake

Here's what you do:

1. Sort the picture cards by word family.

2. Match each word card to its picture.

3. Check.

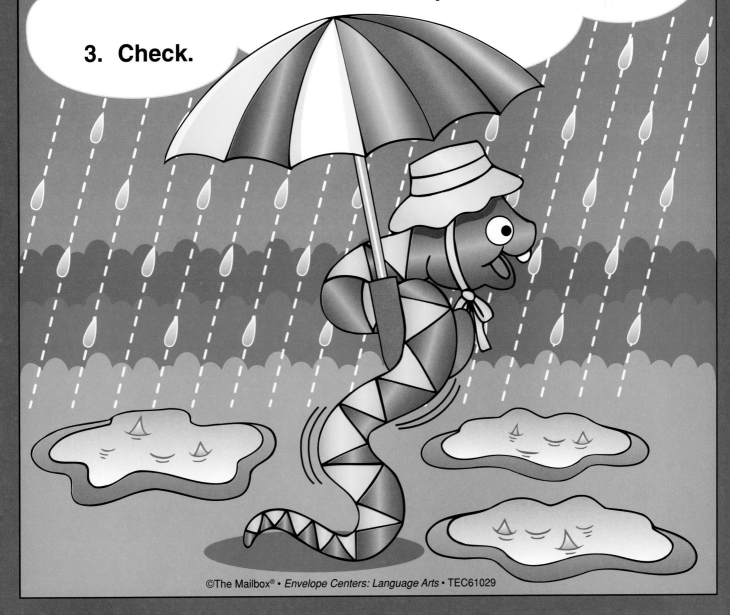

Rainy Day Snake

-ake

-ain

Rainy Day Snake

chain	brain	train
lake	rake	cake

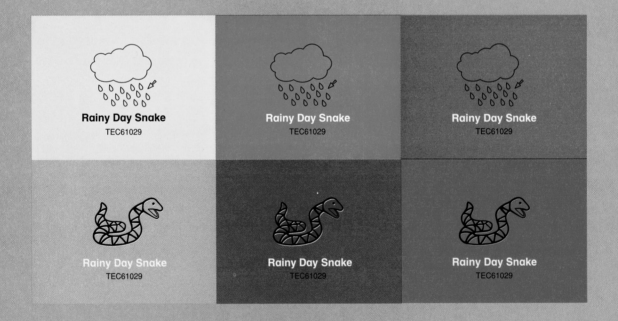

Mice on the Vine

Pages 121–128

Materials:

scissors
glue
10" x 13" envelope
resealable plastic bag

Preparing the center:

1. Tear out the student directions, center mat, and center cards on pages 123–128.
2. Glue the student directions (page 123) on the envelope. If desired, laminate the center mat and cards on pages 125–128.
3. Cut out the cards and place them in the bag.
4. Make copies of the reproducible practice page on page 122.
5. Store the center mat, bag, and copies of the practice page inside the envelope.

Using the center:

Have the student follow the directions on the envelope. Provide assistance as needed. After she completes the center activity, have the student complete a copy of the practice page.

121

Mice on the Vine

Cut.

Glue to match the word family.

Write.

-ice

-ine

Note to the teacher: Use with the directions on page 121.

Mice on the Vine

Here's what you do:

1. Sort the picture cards by word family.

2. Match each word card to its picture.

3. Check.

Mice on the Vine

-ine

-ice

Mice on the Vine

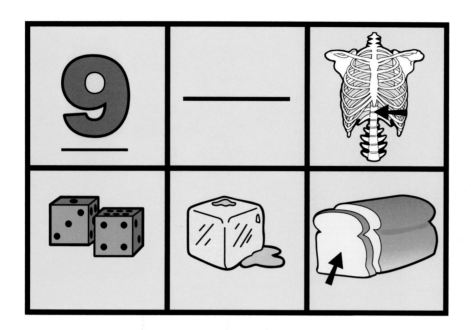

nine	line	spine
dice	ice	slice

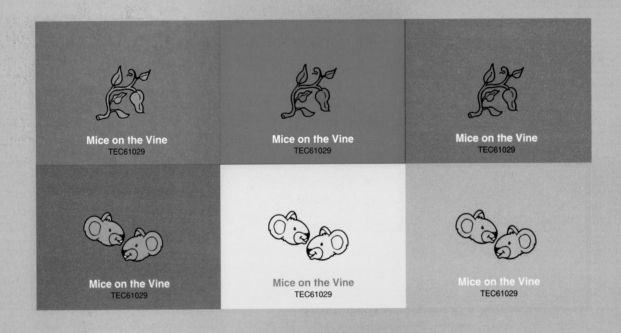